Who were the first North Americans?

Philippa Wingate & Struan Reid

Illustrated by David Cuzik

Designed by Vicki Groombridge

History consultant: Michael Johnson
Series editors: Jane Chisholm & Phil Roxbee Cox

CONTENTS

Who were the first North Americans?

People we now call the Native North Americans. They lived in what has become the United States of America and Canada. This was thousands of years before anybody arrived from Europe. But they hadn't always lived there.

These people are heading toward North America.

A tired child

This map shows the areas of North America in which people settled.

This is the Bering Straits.

Totem poles

Tribes that lived in this blue area are named the Northwest Coast tribes.

Where did they come from?

A part of the world named Asia. Some of the people who lived there walked across to America.

Didn't they have to cross an ocean?

No. At that time Asia and America were joined by a bridge of land and ice. Later, this bridge of land disappeared under a stretch of water now named the Bering Straits. After that, people had to cross to North America in boats.

These people are crossing the sea in canoes made form animal skins.

What are these?

These things probably belonged to some of the first people from Asia to cross into America. Can you guess what they were used for?

These points have been sharpened.

Why did they go to America?

Probably to look for food. They may have been looking for new hunting grounds, and followed herds of animals over the bridge of land. When people got there they loved it, because there was nobody else hunting the same animals.

Map labels:

An igloo

A seal

The people known as the Inuit stayed in the far north.

An elk

A wigwam

Tepees

An earth mound

Buffalo

The people who lived in this green area are known as the Woodland tribes.

Tribes that settled in this yellow area are named Plains Indians.

A Pueblo village

Clay pots

Tribes that settled in this orange area are known as Pueblos.

An Inuit fishing on the ice

What animals did they hunt?

Mainly mammoths and mastodons. These were huge animals, much bigger than elephants.

These men are killing a mammoth with spears.

How long ago did they arrive in North America?

Probably more than 15,000 years ago, at a time when large areas of the Earth's surface was covered in snow and ice.

Did they stay in the north?

No. People went off in different directions. Some moved south to the areas now named Florida and Mexico. Some went to the great forests in the east. Others made their homes on the grassy plains in the middle of North America. Only a few people stayed in the north and northwest.

What did they look like?

Many of them had straight, dark hair and dark eyes. But there were lots of tribes and not all of them looked the same. The shade of their skins varied from light brown to very dark brown.

Did they have different hairstyles?

Yes. Long braids decorated with animal fur or feathers were popular. But some tribes in the east shaved their heads, leaving only a tuft of hair in the middle.

Did they grow beards?

Well the women didn't! Inuit men grew beards to keep them warm. But Plains Indians rarely had them. They plucked out any hair that grew on their bodies. Ouch!

Parka

This man is wearing a headdress with buffalo horns.

This Inuit baby is keeping warm.

Pipe

This man's shirt is decorated with porcupine quills.

This man from the Woodland Mahican tribe has shaved the sides of his head.

Fur boots

Leather leggings

This Navajo hunter is wearing leather boots.

This boy loves his new headdress.

This Plains Indian is carrying her baby on a wooden cradleboard.

These leather shoes are called moccasins. Some tribes had special patterns on their moccasins.

This woman is wearing a dress made from the skin of an elk.

What did they wear?

That depended on where they lived. The Inuit, who lived in cold areas, wore coats called parkas made of seal skins. Plains Indians and Woodland tribes wore long dresses, leggings, shirts, loin cloths and belts made of leather.

For special occasions, they painted patterns on their clothes and decorated them with porcupine quills, beads and tufts of horsehair.

People from Pueblo tribes wore clothes made of cotton or wool.

How did they make clothes out of leather?

They stretched out animal skins on the ground and scraped off any flesh or fur. Then they rubbed the skins with paste made from animals' livers and brains. This made them soft and stopped them from rotting. For special clothes, women chewed pieces of leather to make them really soft.

This woman is scraping clean the skin of an elk.

Wooden stakes

The skin is a little smelly.

This woman is sewing a leather shirt. She enjoys her work.

Quill beads

Horsehair tassels

This shirt has been decorated with beads and dyes.

What ornaments did they wear?

Plenty of different kinds. Both men and women wore ornaments to look beautiful and to show how important they were. Earrings and bracelets made of shells, quills and beads were very popular. Some hunters wore necklaces made from the teeth or claws of animals they had killed.

A bone necklace

Arm bracelets

Shells

A bear claw necklace

A blue stone called turquoise

Feathers

Some men wore rings like these in their noses.

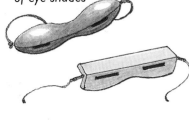
5

Did they build towns?

Yes. Some of the first major towns in North America were built by the people who lived in the eastern woodlands. They settled down there about 3000 years ago.

What were these towns like?

They had large flat-topped mounds built out of earth in the middle of them. These were surrounded by lots of houses and fields where crops were grown.

    The biggest of these settlements was a city called Cahokia. It had over one hundred earth mounds.

This picture shows what one of the first towns would have looked like.

An mound of earth

The chief's house

Food is kept up here, away from mice and rats.

These men are complaining about the hot weather.

These women are weaving.

Tonight's feast

This dog wants the bird for his own dinner.

These men are busy weeding the field.

A farmer's house

The chief is being carried by his servants.

Bowing to the chief

Fields of maize

Fire

A potter at work

This man has hurt his leg and is begging for food.

This man is carrying a very heavy basket.

What was on top of the mounds?

Lots of different important buildings. There were temples, where religious ceremonies took place, and houses, where chiefs and religious leaders lived.

A religious ceremony is taking place in the temple on top of this mound.

A wooden fence

An afternoon nap

A thief

A house cut away so that you can see inside.

How do we know about the towns?

Because you can still see the mounds of earth today. Archeologists have uncovered tombs inside some of them. They found people buried with necklaces, bracelets and pipes. This helped them learn more about what people used to wear.

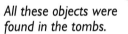

All these objects were found in the tombs.

Who was in charge?

A chief. The Natchez tribe named their chief "the Great Sun". He was very powerful and was carried around the city by his servants. When he died, his wife and servants were killed and buried with him. They must have been worried when he felt ill!

What is this?

It's a mound of earth called the Serpent Mound. People used to worship a spirit here 3000 years ago.

What were their houses like?

That depended on where they lived. The Inuit made houses of ice or stones, earth and whale ribs. Woodland tribes lived in houses made out of tree bark. The Plains Indians lived in tents called tepees.

This igloo is made from blocks of ice glued together with snow.

This woman is warm and cosy inside the igloo.

An oil lamp

Animal skins

A clear ice window

This house is made of the bark of a birch tree.

The side of this igloo has been cut away so that you can see in.

Grass mat

This wooden house from the northwest coast of America has been brightly painted.

This man is filling a hole with snow.

Platform for sleeping on

This underground entrance stops cold air from getting into the igloo.

Was it dark inside their houses?

Yes very. Most tribes only had a fire in the middle of their homes to provide both light and heat.

Inuit had lamps that burned fat from whales. Sometimes they made windows for their igloos from pieces of clear ice.

This man is checking that the dogs have not run off.

This dog is not planning to run anywhere.

Did they decorate their houses?

Some were painted with patterns, or pictures of animal spirits. People believed that these spirits protected the family who lived in the house.

On the walls inside, some people hung weapons, ceremonial masks and blankets. But most families had very little furniture.

8

Is there a difference between a tepee and a wigwam?

Yes. Tepees were cone-shaped houses made with poles covered in animal skins. They could be put up and taken down quickly. Horses dragged the poles when a tribe moved their home. Wigwams were cone-shaped houses too, but instead of skins, they were covered with tree bark.

Did they have toilets?

No. They had to make do with the great outdoors. Not much fun in the snow!

Women usually put up the tepees.

Each tepee needed about 12 long wooden poles.

The poles were tied in a cone shape.

About 15 buffalo skins were sewn together to make a tepee covering.

The skins were stretched over the poles.

This is where smoke from the fire escaped.

This tepee has been painted with bright dyes.

The pattern on this tepee shows that the family belongs to the Cheyenne tribe.

The door of a tepee always faced the rising sun in the east.

A backrest made of willow sticks

This baby has decided to explore.

These women are struggling to unroll the buffalo skins.

Did you know?

Native North Americans had saunas, called sweat lodges. Inside, hot stones were sprinkled with water to make steam. This made people sweat, getting rid of grease and dirt on their skin.

Two sweaty men in a sweat lodge

9

How big was a tribe?

All different sizes. Inuit lived in small family groups of 10 or 20 people. But some tribes, such as the Sioux on the Great Plains, had thousands of members, living in groups of up to 300.

Members of the Iroquois tribe gather for a meeting called a Powwow.

These women are preparing food for the people who have come to the Powwow.

A greedy boy secretly helping himself to food

Did tribes have kings?

No. But they had chiefs who were chosen for their bravery or wisdom. Some chiefs were very powerful. They decided when their tribe would fight a war or move camp. Others just gave advice on farming and hunting.

The chiefs are listening to stories about last year.

Hunters have killed a deer to add to the feast.

These chiefs are exchanging gifts.

Did they have governments?

Not really. But people, such as the Woodland tribe called the Iroquois, had councils of wise men who met to make important decisions. They laid down strict rules about hunting, war, and religion which all the members of the tribe had to follow.

What was a Powwow?

A meeting held every summer by the members of large tribes. The chiefs told stories about what had happened to their people during the year.

During a Powwow, there were athletic competitions and dancing, and religious ceremonies performed by medicine men.

Who were medicine men?

Important members of tribes. As well as leading religious ceremonies, they healed wounds and illnesses using magic spells and medicines made from plants. They carried medicine bundles or bags filled with special objects that they believed gave them power to cure people.

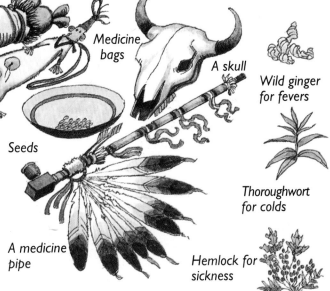

Medicine bags

A skull

Wild ginger for fevers

Seeds

Thoroughwort for colds

A medicine pipe

Hemlock for sickness

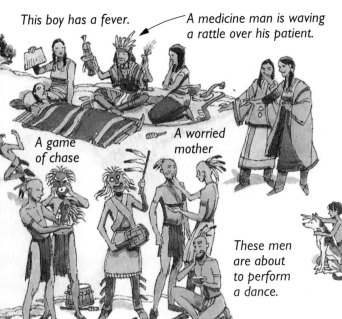

This boy has a fever.

A medicine man is waving a rattle over his patient.

A game of chase

A worried mother

These men are about to perform a dance.

Did tribes have policemen?

Sort of. The warriors were in charge of capturing and punishing anybody who committed a crime against the tribe.

How were criminals punished?

Most were ignored. Nobody in the camp would talk to them or even look at them. In some tribes, a murderer would be tried by the chief and his council. If found guilty, the murderer had to walk away from the trial and four executioners would shoot arrows at him.

Did you know?

Native North Americans weren't always given names at birth. They had names, such as Long Ears or Pale Eyes. Later, they were sometimes given new names which described big events in their lives, such as *Kills Two Eagles* or *Runs from Bear*.

This man has been caught stealing.

The chief decides his punishment.

Did they all speak the same language?

Not all of them. In fact there were about a thousand different languages. But they had other ways of communicating with different tribes. They made signals with their fingers and hands.

What were these signals like?

That depends on what they wanted to say. Here are a few examples.

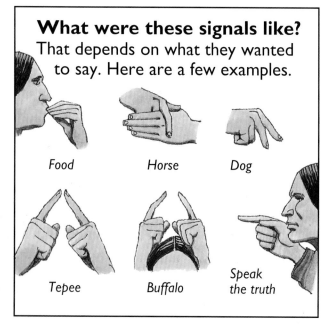

Food

Horse

Dog

Tepee

Buffalo

Speak the truth

Could they read and write?

No. But some tribes used a kind of picture writing to record great battles and successful hunting expeditions. They drew this picture writing on animal skins.

The symbols below are picture writing.

This tepee with two arrows tells of a village where everyone was killed.

This picture appears in a story of a man who stole 30 spotted ponies.

This picture shows a chief wearing a feather and holding a pipe.

What were smoke signals?

People used the smoke from fires to send warnings over long distances. They made patterns in the smoke by covering the fire with a blanket and then removing it.

They could also send messages by flashing shiny pieces of metal in the sunlight. By arranging sticks and stones in patterns on the ground, hunters on the move could leave messages for anyone following them.

These people are following a hunting party. They are guided by signals that have been left for them.

This dog is eager to get going.

This woman thinks that she knows the way.

This shows the direction the hunters have taken.

This man is flashing a piece of metal.

How did they get around?

Mostly on foot. They only had horses after people brought them from Europe. The Native North Americans soon became great riders. The Sioux called horses "shunka wakan", which means "sacred dogs".

Some tribes used horses and dogs to pull a type of sled called a "travois". These were made from two tepee poles tied together.

A travois pulled by a horse

A small travois pulled by a dog

Tepee poles

A heavy pack

These Inuit have put their heavy packs on wooden sleds.

This dog wishes that he had snow shoes.

A small child with big snow shoes to stop her sinking into the snow.

Did they have wagons?

No. Wagons have wheels and the Native North Americans never invented wheels. Most tribes carried things in packs on their backs. In the far north, the Inuit used sleds pulled by dogs to cross the snow.

A pair of snow shoes

What about ships?

They didn't have anything as big as a ship. But they did have canoes. They made them out of wood and bark and decorated them with carvings or pictures of animals.

It's this man's turn to pull the canoe ashore.

These canoes are made of animal skins and have been painted.

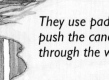

They use paddles to push the canoes through the water.

Did they really say "How"?

Sort of. Some Plains Indians greeted people with the words "Hau kola" which means "Hello friend". The Europeans who went to North America may have shortened this to "Hau".

13

What did they hunt?

That depended on where they lived. The tribes who lived on the Great Plains mostly hunted buffalo (also called bison). The hunters had to make special preparations before going on a buffalo hunt.

What did they do?

They performed a Buffalo Dance. Some dancers put on large animal masks, while others pretended to try to kill them. It was their way of asking for good luck on a hunting trip.

These men are doing a Buffalo Dance.

There are thousands of buffalo in this herd.

This man has lost his disguise in the excitement.

A wolf disguise

They use spears to kill the buffalo.

This man is famous for being a fast runner and a good shot.

The buffalo are falling over the cliff. It's a long way down!

How did they kill the buffalo?

With spears or bows and arrows. The hunters followed the buffalo, creeping up on them disguised as wolves. Sometimes hunters drove whole herds over clifftops so that the animals were killed by the fall.

This man is collecting a dead buffalo.

This man would rather be hunting.

These men are cutting up the dead buffalo.

This man is lazy.

Was all the meat eaten at once?

Most of it, but some had to be saved for winter. Women cut the meat into strips and hung it up in the sun to dry, or smoked it over a fire. Sometimes they mixed it with dried fruit to make a tasty food called "pemmican".

What did other tribes hunt?

Woodland tribes hunted moose, deer, beavers and bears. If he was quiet enough, a hunter could paddle his canoe right up to an animal drinking from a lake or stream and spear it.

Inuits in the north hunted seals and whales and caught fish through holes in the ice.

A lucky Inuit hunter with his harpoon

A hungry hunter

A thirsty elk

An unlucky seal

Did you know?

Before European settlers brought metal pots to America, the Sioux tribe cooked their stews in buffalo stomachs.

A buffalo stomach

What else did they eat?

Tribes who settled in one place grew crops such as pumpkins and artichokes. Most important was Indian corn and maize.

Hunting tribes, that moved from one place to another, also picked wild plants, like turnips, onions, cherries, plums, berries and herbs.

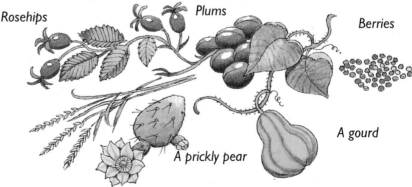

Rosehips

Plums

Berries

A prickly pear

A gourd

15

Where did they buy things?

Not from shops or stores. They didn't have any. People would travel from miles around to buy and sell things at a regular meeting place. Some Woodland tribes had a kind of shell money called "wampum". But most tribes swapped their goods for things that they wanted.

Did they trade with white people?

Yes. When Europeans came to North America (see page 26), many tribes traded with them. The Europeans brought guns, knives, cloth and blankets, which they swapped in return for furs.

These Native North Americans have come to see what the French traders are selling.

Did they make things to trade?

Yes. Lots of different things. Baskets decorated with shells and feathers were made from brightly dyed grasses. They used flattened porcupine quills and glass beads from the white traders, to sew onto clothes and bags. Many Pueblo tribes made beautiful clay pots which they painted with red, yellow and black dyes.

This is a Pueblo village, where many people are making things to use and trade.

A loom, used to make cotton cloth

A nasty fall

This woman is painting a pot.

Clay coil pots

The ladders are used to get up to the houses.

This hairstyle is worn by many Pueblo women.

To keep out enemies, there are no doors on the ground floor.

A selection of clay pots and leather bags made by Native North Americans

This bird carved from wood is used for hunting.

This bag, made for carrying food, is decorated with porcupine quills.

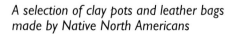

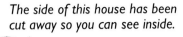
The side of this house has been cut away so you can see inside.

Repairing the wall

The houses are made of dried mud.

This man thinks that he's waving to his brother.

A pot about to be dropped

Pots are baked in these fires.

A man taking a nap, in the hot afternoon sun

This is a raven totem, carved on the top of the totem pole.

This carving shows a monster, called the clam. It was said to live underwater and sucked in all the canoes passing over it.

This is an eagle totem. Many tribes tell of a man who fed eagles. In return, they helped him when he was in trouble.

This is an owl totem. There is a folk tale of a woman who was turned into an owl as a punishment for her selfishness.

This beaver totem is holding a stick in its front paws and gnawing it.

How did they make pots?

They coiled around thin rolls of clay and then smoothed out the bumpy sides. After drying the pots in the sun, they decorated them. Finally, the pots were baked in a fire to make them hard.

These Pueblo pots are painted with bold patterns.

What were totem poles?

Tall wooden poles with carvings of animals and birds. Each creature, called a totem, had its own meaning or story.

Totem poles were made by tribes on the northwest coast. The poles usually stood outside houses, telling the history of the family inside.

A wolf totem is carved at the bottom of this pole.

17

What did they do for fun?

The same kinds of things we still do today, such as playing sports and games, singing, dancing and telling stories. Life was hard, but the Native North Americans always found time to enjoy themselves.

This is a ball game called lacrosse. Sometimes hundreds of people joined in.

Did they gamble?

Yes. They placed bets on almost anything. They gambled on the outcome of horse races, team games and even spear throwing competitions.

Gamblers

This woman is not enjoying the game.

Foul!

This man is sure his team will win.

A bump on the head

These men are hitting each other, not the ball.

This man is not taking a rest.

Watch out!

These players disagree on the rules.

This man has forgotten it is a game.

What games did children play?

Mostly games that taught them how to hunt and fight. Boys learned to ride on wooden horses. In winter, children made toboggans and went for rides in the snow.

These ducks are carved from walrus tusks.

What kind of sports did they play?

All sorts, including horse racing, archery contests and ball games. Woodland tribes played a game now known as "lacrosse". Using sticks with baskets attached to them, the players hurled a ball, made from the skin of a deer, through high goal posts.

This hoop game helps the boys learn to throw spears.

18

Did they have story books?

Not books, but people loved to tell stories. It was an important way of passing on information about a tribe's history and customs. Many stories taught children to respect animals and nature.

Why is this man going the wrong way?

Goal posts

What about dancing?

They loved it. Many religious ceremonies included dances. Pueblo tribes danced with rattles tied to their legs. The Plain Indians did dances to worship spirits.

1. This man is doing the Eagle Dance. He runs in.

2. He circles around and around.

3. He jumps up.

4. Finally, the dancer falls down like a dying eagle.

Did they like music?

Yes, but they didn't have CDs and cassettes. They made their own music, beating out rhythms on drums or shaking rattles. Some rattles were made from the dried shells of fruit, filled with pebbles or seeds. Others were made from tortoise shells. Some tribes played flutes and whistles made of wood or bone.

A drum

A turtle shell rattle

A hand drum

Horsehair

A flute

Rattles

Did you know?

Instead of fighting, two angry Inuit would insult each other in songs. It was up to their audience to judge which of them was rudest. The rudest one was the winner.

A blush

This man is so insulting.

Did they believe in God?

Not exactly. The Native North Americans believed that everything in the world had a soul or spirit. Spirits were very powerful and could help or harm human beings, so they had to be treated with great respect.

Where did these spirits live?

The most important spirits, called Holy People, lived above the sky. Others lived in rivers, mountains, trees and lakes. Spirits dashed around the world on sunbeams or rainbows, or on flashes of lightning.

Sometimes people wore masks like these to look like spirits.

This mask, from the northwest coast of America, is the spirit of the Nootka bird.

Did different tribes worship different spirits?

Yes. The Apaches believed in a spirit called the Changing Woman. She made people and taught them how to live in peace. The Sioux prayed to the Wakan Tanka, a spirit that controlled everything around them. Many tribes believed in a Thunderbird. You can read a story about a Thunderbird on page 31.

What is a Thunderbird?

A spirit in the shape of a great bird. It produced thunder when it flapped its wings, and lightning when it opened and closed its eyes. You can make a Thunderbird mobile.

2. Paint both sides of the bird.

1. Draw a Thunderbird shape on a piece of cardboard and cut it out.

3. Hang your bird from a piece of thread.

Did they have religious ceremonies?

Lots of them. At certain times of the year they gave thanks to spirits. People dressed in special costumes, painted their clothes and bodies and performed special dances.

These three men are doing the Dance of the Mountain Spirits.

Did they really do Rain Dances?

Pueblo tribes did them to ask spirits for rain for their crops. Another famous dance was called the Sun Dance. Plains Indians pushed skewers through the skin on their chests. The skewers were attached to a pole by ropes. Ignoring the pain, they danced until they were exhausted.

These men are blowing whistles made from eagle bones.

A buffalo skull

Singers

Did they believe in ghosts?

Yes. They believed that the ghost of anyone they had upset would haunt them. Sometimes a dead person's home was pulled down to stop their ghost from haunting it.

Young warriors performing the Sun Dance in a special building called a lodge.

This man likes the sound of his own voice.

The men hold an eagle feather in each hand.

These men have skewers in their chests.

This man is growing tired.

This man is calling to the spirits.

This woman cannot watch. She doesn't like blood.

Did they have an army?

No, but each tribe had warriors, known as braves. Their job was to fight and protect their village.

Most wars between tribes were about horses or hunting territory. But later, when Europeans arrived in North America and began to take the land, many braves fought to stop them.

The Crow tribe's camp

This man is ready for a fight.

Sioux warriors are attacking the Crow tribe who have stolen some of their horses.

This isn't a giant walking stick, but something called a coup stick.

This brave isn't feeling very brave.

This man is a good rider. He can gallop on his horse without a saddle.

This horse is wearing war paint.

Did they have guns?

Not until people brought them over from Europe. Most tribes fought with wooden bows and arrows. You can see many of their weapons on these pages, including spears, knives, clubs and a kind of hatchet called a tomahawk.

A quiver of arrows

A bow

A tomahawk

A hammer

A spear

What is a coup stick?

Warriors believed that to touch a man with a stick and steal his weapons was braver than just killing him.

A Sioux coup stick

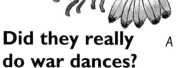

A peace pipe

Did braves really scalp people?

Yes. It was really horrid. Sometimes a warrior sewed a scalp to his war shirt. It was his way of showing his friends how good he was at fighting.

Did they wear war paint?

Yes, they covered their clothes, bodies, horses and weapons with vivid patterns. They believed that this would protect them in battle.

Did they really do war dances?

Yes, before and after battles. They asked spirits for courage and celebrated victories. When peace was made, they smoked a peace pipe. They believed that the smoke took their prayers to the spirits.

These warriors are riding and shooting in time with each other.

This old warrior has an impressive war bonnet

This man is using a tomahawk.

This horse doesn't like violence. It's going home.

Did they get medals for bravery?

No, but Sioux warriors were given eagle feathers for brave deeds. Some braves wore war bonnets with up to a hundred feathers.

These are some of the feathers a brave could win.

This warrior is about to be scalped.

A spot means an enemy killed

Wounded many times

Taken a scalp

This man has been busy!

23

Who were the first European visitors?

A group of people from Scandinavia called the Vikings. They arrived in North America about a thousand years ago.

For many years people thought that an Italian called Christopher Columbus was the first European to reach America. But experts have now discovered that the Vikings got there 500 years before him.

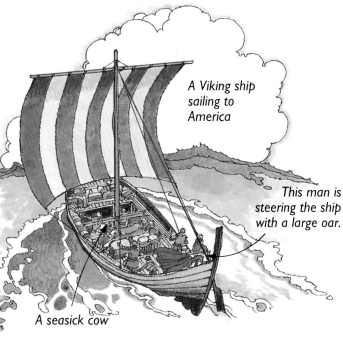

This map shows the routes taken by the Vikings and by Columbus and his crew.

A Viking ship sailing to America

This man is steering the ship with a large oar.

A seasick cow

Where did the Vikings land?

In a place now called L'Anse aux Meadows, which is on an island now called Newfoundland, in Canada. Archeologists know this because they have discovered the remains of Viking houses in Newfoundland.

The chief

Why did the Vikings go there?

By mistake really. The first Viking to see North America was on his way to an island called Greenland. His ship was blown way off course by a terrible storm.

When he told the people on Greenland what he had seen, some decided to set off to explore the new land.

Did the Vikings stay in America?

At first. But soon they began to quarrel with the Native North Americans. When fights broke out between them, the Vikings sailed home.

These braves are chasing away a group of Viking settlers.

So what about Columbus?

He set sail from Spain in 1492, with an expedition of three ships. They sailed west searching for China. When land was finally spotted, Columbus thought he was in the Indian Ocean. But he was wrong.

So where did he land?

On a group of islands now called the Bahamas, off the American coast. Columbus is famous for reaching America because he was followed by many Europeans who then settled there.

This picture shows Columbus and his crew arriving on the shores of the Bahamas.

This is Columbus's ship, called the "Santa Maria".

These men have taken their canoe to look at the ships.

The "Niña"

The "Pinta"

A Spanish flag

This man is ready for a fight.

This man wants to go back to the ship.

Columbus

Women have food for the visitors. But the chief looks suspicious.

This man is not very interested by the visitors.

Why are Native North Americans called Redskins?

Early visitors to North America came across people in Newfoundland who painted their clothes and bodies with with bright red dye. They became known as Redskins.

Brightly painted men

Who were the first European settlers?

People from all over Europe who arrived in North America about a hundred years after Columbus. They built settlements on the east coast.

A lookout

A lost hat

These panicky people have climbed into a lifeboat.

This woman is feeling very sick.

Man overboard!

This stowaway is hiding behind some barrels.

Food supplies

Why did they go to America?

They thought life would be better there. Some of them were farmers who wanted their own land. Many were people whose religious beliefs were unpopular in their home lands. Among these religious people were the Pilgrim Fathers.

This woman is trying to get on with her cooking.

The families sleep below deck during the voyage.

This is where the rats sleep.

This man is dreaming of England and dry land.

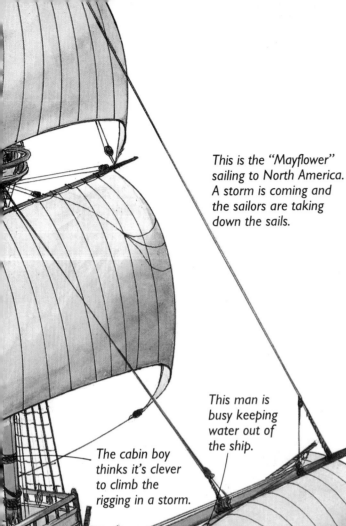

This is the "Mayflower" sailing to North America. A storm is coming and the sailors are taking down the sails.

This man is busy keeping water out of the ship.

The cabin boy thinks it's clever to climb the rigging in a storm.

Who were the Pilgrim Fathers?

A group of English people who followed a religion called Puritanism. They wanted to be free to follow their religion, so they sailed to America in a ship called the "Mayflower". When they arrived, they settled down and built a town.

Did the Pilgrim Fathers meet any Native North Americans?

Yes. Some tribes helped the settlers. During their first winter in America, many of the Pilgrim Fathers died of starvation. The Native North Americans taught them how to plant corn, hunt and fish.

Did any of the Pilgrims survive the winter?

Yes. Although almost half of them died. The survivors had a big feast with their Native North American friends to celebrate. They baked bread with the corn from their first harvest. Every year, this event is still marked by many people with a special Thanksgiving meal.

Did you know?

The settlers brought with them diseases like measles and the common cold. Native North Americans had never had these diseases before, so they became very ill. Some tribes were almost wiped out.

The Pilgrims dressed in very plain clothes.

Native North Americans bring a deer to eat at the feast.

Did the Europeans stay?

Yes. More and more of them arrived in North America. They settled down and built farms and towns. They took large areas of land for themselves and put up fences around it. Later, they even built a railway across the Great Plains. These people are known as White Americans.

Did the White Americans buy land from tribes?

Some people tried to, but many tribes thought that land was like air or water. It didn't belong to anyone and they couldn't sell something they didn't own.

Most settlers just took any land that they wanted.

Did any tribes fight the White Americans?

Yes. Native North Americans decided they had to stop white people stealing land. Battles were fought all over North America and the fighting continued for many years.

This fort is being attacked by a Woodland tribe.

More soldiers are on their way. They probably won't be here in time.

This brave has climbed up to cut down the flag.

Did you know?

White Americans slaughtered millions of buffalo. In 1850, there were over 60 million buffalo on the Great Plains. After 40 years, there were only 550 left. Without buffalo to hunt, many tribes starved.

A White American killing buffalo with his gun

A safe place to fire from

These men have been drinking, not fighting.

These children are trying to be brave, but they are very frightened.

The canon is rolled up this ramp.

Hand-to-hand combat

Did Native North American women fight?

Yes, in some tribes. They defended the camps while the men were away fighting. Some women did a Ghost Dance. They believed that if their dancing pleased the spirits it would make white people go and the buffalo return.

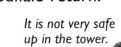

These women are doing a Ghost Dance.

What is this?

A ghost shirt. Warriors thought that these shirts could protect them from white people's bullets. But in one battle 300 Sioux were killed, including some men wearing ghost shirts. After this, the Native North Americans realized that they would never defeat the white people.

A Sioux ghost shirt

It is not very safe up in the tower.

Braves are climbing over the walls and on top of the huts.

It takes a long time to reload these rifles.

Sleeping quarters. Cut away so you can see inside.

A badly wounded man

These soldiers are shooting braves as they come through the gate.

Braves have broken through the main gate.

Who won the war?

The White Americans. By 1890, all the Native North American tribes were defeated and their weapons taken away.

What happened to the Native North Americans?

About a hundred years ago, many tribes were rounded up and taken to live on special areas of land called reservations.

Sometimes the reservations were on their own land, but some tribes were forced to leave their homelands altogether.

White American soldiers are taking this tribe to a reservation.

Was the land ever given back?

Only some of it. The Sioux, for example, are still asking the US government to give them back an area called the Black Hills in South Dakota. The government have offered them money for the hills. But the Sioux believe that the land is sacred and not for sale.

The Black Hills

What were the reservations like?

Some were on good land, with hunting grounds and forests. But others were on poor land that White Americans didn't want.

Sometimes dancing and religious ceremonies were forbidden. A few tribes were even discouraged from speaking their own language.

This family have made their home out of tree trunks.

Do they still live on reservations?

Yes. Many Native North Americans have chosen to stay on reservations, but many also live in towns and cities.

They lead modern lives, living in houses, driving cars and running their own businesses. But many people still attend Powwows each summer to keep alive Native North American ways and customs.

Members of the Oglala tribe have gathered at a summer Powwow.

People are watching attentively.

The owner of this truck won't be pleased to find it being used as a seat.

This dancer is unsure of the steps.

Men dancing with Sunburst bustles made of feathers on their backs

In search of the Thunderbird

At the top of many totem poles there is the carving of a mighty bird, with an eagle's beak and piercing eyes. This is the myth of what that bird is, and how its totem was made.

A boy named Little Nose lived in a village by the sea. He loved to watch the totem pole carvers at work and longed to join them. They laughed, saying "If you can carve the Thunderbird, we'll let you carve your own poles." This was a trick, for no-one had ever seen the creature that caused the sound of thunder. But the boy decided to find the Thunderbird.

Little Nose set off in his canoe. Once, he heard thunder up ahead but, before he could reach it, another thunder clap sounded farther away. However hard he tried, Little Nose could never catch up with the thunder. After many days, he decided to return home. As he paddled, the water grew rough and an enormous killer whale swam by. Suddenly the sky was filled by a terrifying bird. The bird was so large that - for a moment - it seemed to blot out the sun. The bird snatched up the whale in its talons. The air rushed through its feathers, sending the sound of thunder through the skies.

Then the mightiest of all birds swooped down to the tiny speck of the boy. "Who are you that you dare to follow me?" it demanded in a booming voice. "Are you the bravest of braves?"

"N-N-No," stammered Little Nose. "I am only a boy who wants to carve you. I want to be a carver of totem poles."

"And so you shall be," replied the bird. Gently lifting the boy and the canoe, he took them back to the village. "You shall grow up to be the greatest carver of them all, but you must promise me one thing." The boy nodded. "You must always carve a likeness of me at the top of every pole." Little Nose agreed gladly. And he kept his word, as all can see.

Index

32

Answer
Page 2.
The objects are spear heads made from a type of stone called flint.

First published in 1995 by Usborne Publishing Ltd, Usborne House, 83-85 Saffron Hill London ECIN 8RT, England.
Copyright © 1995 Usborne Publishing Ltd.

The name Usborne and the device are Trade Marks of Usborne Publishing Ltd.
First published in America in August 1995
Printed in Belgium